The Homeschool Planner

ISBN: 978-1-910713-44-0

Published by Pink Elephant Publications

The Homeschool Planner is the perfect solution to all your homeschool planning needs. Whether you are a homeschooling newbie or an experienced homeschooling parent, this planner is designed to make your year, month, and weekly planning as effortless and enjoyable as possible. With room to plan and record progress and achievements for up to 4 individual students, the planner will allow you to stay focused, and organize efficiently as you develop your homeschooling techniques. The planner is undated for adaptability and convenience.

Inside your planner you will find:

Yearly Planner - Plan ahead of time with a yearly calendar by making notes of key dates, important holidays and upcoming events.

Website & Password Tracker - Keep a record of all those crucial online educational resource websites and login information.

Attendance Record & Student Information – Record attendance, school years, and grades for each student.

Book List – Make a list of student-specific book names, authors and subjects.

Supplies and To-do List – Make a list of everything you need all in one place.

After School Activity Planner – Plan days, times and places for each individual student's activities.

Field Trip Planner – Plan those all-important field trips, with space to note dates, places, and details to remember.

School Year Preparation Planner – Plan lessons ahead of time for each subject.

Yearly Goals - Set academic and personal goals for you and all your students.

Monthly Planner - Map out the months in more detail. These pages are undated with fillable fields for your convenience.

Weekly Planner - Plan student-specific timetables in advance or record the day's accomplishments later – the choice is yours.

Grades & Milestones - Keep track of all those important achievements.

Year in Review – Reflect on the past year and brainstorm for the year ahead.

Planner Contents

YEAR:

Yearly Planner

Year:

SEPTEMBER	OCTOBER

JANUARY	FEBRUARY

MAY	JUNE

YEAR:

This is our year to...

NOVEMBER	DECEMBER

MARCH	APRIL

JULY	AUGUST

WEBSITES / PASSWORDS

Website & Password Tracker

WEBSITE	USERNAME	PASSWORD
		☆☆☆☆☆☆

Student Details

NAME:

SCHOOL YEAR:

GRADE:

NAME:

SCHOOL YEAR:

GRADE:

NAME:

SCHOOL YEAR:

GRADE:

NAME:

SCHOOL YEAR:

GRADE:

ATTENDANCE

	SEPTEMBER				OCTOBER				NOVEMBER				DECEMBER				JANUARY				FEBRUARY			
	1	2	3	4	1	2	3	4	1	2	3	4	1	2	3	4	1	2	3	4	1	2	3	4
1																								
2																								
3																								
4																								
5																								
6																								
7																								
8																								
9																								
10																								
11																								
12																								
13																								
14																								
15																								
16																								
17																								
18																								
19																								
20																								
21																								
22																								
23																								
24																								
25																								
26																								
27																								
28																								
29																								
30																								
31																								
TOTAL:																								

1 2 3 4

ATTENDANCE

	MARCH				APRIL				MAY				JUNE				JULY				AUGUST			
	1	2	3	4	1	2	3	4	1	2	3	4	1	2	3	4	1	2	3	4	1	2	3	4
1																								
2																								
3																								
4																								
5																								
6																								
7																								
8																								
9																								
10																								
11																								
12																								
13																								
14																								
15																								
16																								
17																								
18																								
19																								
20																								
21																								
22																								
23																								
24																								
25																								
26																								
27																								
28																								
29																								
30																								
31																								
TOTAL:																								

BOOK LIST

BOOK NAME	AUTHOR	SUBJECT	STUDENT

Supplies & To-Do List

SUPPLIES NEEDED	TO DO

SUPPLIES / TO-DO LIST

ACTIVITIES

DAY	TIME	PLACE

DAY	TIME	PLACE

DAY	TIME	PLACE

DAY	TIME	PLACE

Field Trip Planner

DATE:	PLACE:	DETAILS:

School Year Preparation

Year: ____________________

SUBJECT:	SUBJECT:
☐	☐
☐	☐
☐	☐
☐	☐
☐	☐

SUBJECT:	SUBJECT:
☐	☐
☐	☐
☐	☐
☐	☐
☐	☐

SUBJECT:	SUBJECT:
☐	☐
☐	☐
☐	☐
☐	☐
☐	☐

ADDITIONAL NOTES:

SUBJECT:	SUBJECT:
☐	☐
☐	☐
☐	☐
☐	☐
☐	☐

SUBJECT:	SUBJECT:
☐	☐
☐	☐
☐	☐
☐	☐
☐	☐

SUBJECT:	SUBJECT:
☐	☐
☐	☐
☐	☐
☐	☐
☐	☐

Yearly Goals

YEAR: ____________________

GROUP GOALS

PERSONAL AND ACADEMIC GOALS FOR:

PERSONAL AND ACADEMIC GOALS FOR:

YEARLY GOALS

Believe you can and you will...

MY GOALS

PERSONAL AND ACADEMIC GOALS FOR:

PERSONAL AND ACADEMIC GOALS FOR:

YEARLY GOALS

Monthly Planner

MONTH:

MONDAY	TUESDAY	WEDNESDAY	THURSDAY

MONTH:

This is our month to...

FRIDAY	SATURDAY	SUNDAY

NOTES

MONTH:

Monthly Planner

MONTH: ____________

MONDAY	TUESDAY	WEDNESDAY	THURSDAY

MONTH:

This is our month to... ____________

FRIDAY	SATURDAY	SUNDAY

NOTES

MONTH:

Monthly Planner

MONTH: ____________________

MONDAY	TUESDAY	WEDNESDAY	THURSDAY

MONTH:

This is our month to...

FRIDAY	SATURDAY	SUNDAY

NOTES

MONTH:

Monthly Planner

MONTH:

MONDAY	TUESDAY	WEDNESDAY	THURSDAY

MONTH:

This is our month to...

FRIDAY	SATURDAY	SUNDAY	NOTES

MONTH:

Monthly Planner

MONTH:

MONDAY	TUESDAY	WEDNESDAY	THURSDAY

MONTH:

This is our month to...

FRIDAY	SATURDAY	SUNDAY

NOTES

MONTH:

Monthly Planner

MONTH:

MONDAY	TUESDAY	WEDNESDAY	THURSDAY

MONTH:

This is our month to...

FRIDAY	SATURDAY	SUNDAY

NOTES

MONTH:

Monthly Planner

MONTH:

MONDAY	TUESDAY	WEDNESDAY	THURSDAY

MONTH:

This is our month to... ______

FRIDAY	SATURDAY	SUNDAY

NOTES

MONTH:

Monthly Planner

MONTH: ______________________

MONDAY	TUESDAY	WEDNESDAY	THURSDAY

MONTH:

This is our month to... ____________

FRIDAY	SATURDAY	SUNDAY

NOTES

MONTH:

Monthly Planner

MONTH:

MONDAY	TUESDAY	WEDNESDAY	THURSDAY

MONTH:

This is our month to... ______________________

FRIDAY	SATURDAY	SUNDAY

NOTES

MONTH:

Monthly Planner

MONTH:

MONDAY	TUESDAY	WEDNESDAY	THURSDAY

MONTH:

This is our month to... ____________________

FRIDAY	SATURDAY	SUNDAY

NOTES

MONTH:

Monthly Planner

MONTH:

MONDAY	TUESDAY	WEDNESDAY	THURSDAY

MONTH:

This is our month to...

FRIDAY	SATURDAY	SUNDAY

NOTES

MONTH:

Monthly Planner

MONTH:

MONDAY	TUESDAY	WEDNESDAY	THURSDAY

MONTH:

This is our month to... ______________________

FRIDAY	SATURDAY	SUNDAY

NOTES

MONTH:

Weekly Planner

WEEK:

	NAME:	NAME:
MONDAY	☐ ☐ ☐ ☐ ☐	☐ ☐ ☐ ☐ ☐
TUESDAY	☐ ☐ ☐ ☐ ☐	☐ ☐ ☐ ☐ ☐
WEDNESDAY	☐ ☐ ☐ ☐ ☐	☐ ☐ ☐ ☐ ☐
THURSDAY	☐ ☐ ☐ ☐ ☐	☐ ☐ ☐ ☐ ☐
FRIDAY	☐ ☐ ☐ ☐ ☐	☐ ☐ ☐ ☐ ☐
SATURDAY	☐ ☐ ☐ ☐ ☐	☐ ☐ ☐ ☐ ☐
SUNDAY	☐ ☐ ☐ ☐ ☐	☐ ☐ ☐ ☐ ☐

WEEK:

This is our week to... ______

NAME:	NAME:
☐ ☐ ☐ ☐ ☐	☐ ☐ ☐ ☐ ☐
☐ ☐ ☐ ☐ ☐	☐ ☐ ☐ ☐ ☐
☐ ☐ ☐ ☐ ☐	☐ ☐ ☐ ☐ ☐
☐ ☐ ☐ ☐ ☐	☐ ☐ ☐ ☐ ☐
☐ ☐ ☐ ☐ ☐	☐ ☐ ☐ ☐ ☐
☐ ☐ ☐ ☐ ☐	☐ ☐ ☐ ☐ ☐
☐ ☐ ☐ ☐ ☐	☐ ☐ ☐ ☐ ☐

SUBJECTS

WEEK:

Weekly Planner

WEEK: ____________________

	NAME:	NAME:
MONDAY	☐ ☐ ☐ ☐ ☐	☐ ☐ ☐ ☐ ☐
TUESDAY	☐ ☐ ☐ ☐ ☐	☐ ☐ ☐ ☐ ☐
WEDNESDAY	☐ ☐ ☐ ☐ ☐	☐ ☐ ☐ ☐ ☐
THURSDAY	☐ ☐ ☐ ☐ ☐	☐ ☐ ☐ ☐ ☐
FRIDAY	☐ ☐ ☐ ☐ ☐	☐ ☐ ☐ ☐ ☐
SATURDAY	☐ ☐ ☐ ☐ ☐	☐ ☐ ☐ ☐ ☐
SUNDAY	☐ ☐ ☐ ☐ ☐	☐ ☐ ☐ ☐ ☐

WEEK:

This is our week to... ______________________

NAME:	NAME:
☐ ☐ ☐ ☐ ☐	☐ ☐ ☐ ☐ ☐
☐ ☐ ☐ ☐ ☐	☐ ☐ ☐ ☐ ☐
☐ ☐ ☐ ☐ ☐	☐ ☐ ☐ ☐ ☐
☐ ☐ ☐ ☐ ☐	☐ ☐ ☐ ☐ ☐
☐ ☐ ☐ ☐ ☐	☐ ☐ ☐ ☐ ☐
☐ ☐ ☐ ☐ ☐	☐ ☐ ☐ ☐ ☐
☐ ☐ ☐ ☐ ☐	☐ ☐ ☐ ☐ ☐

SUBJECTS

WEEK:

Weekly Planner

WEEK: ______

	NAME:	NAME:
MONDAY	☐ ☐ ☐ ☐ ☐	☐ ☐ ☐ ☐ ☐
TUESDAY	☐ ☐ ☐ ☐ ☐	☐ ☐ ☐ ☐ ☐
WEDNESDAY	☐ ☐ ☐ ☐ ☐	☐ ☐ ☐ ☐ ☐
THURSDAY	☐ ☐ ☐ ☐ ☐	☐ ☐ ☐ ☐ ☐
FRIDAY	☐ ☐ ☐ ☐ ☐	☐ ☐ ☐ ☐ ☐
SATURDAY	☐ ☐ ☐ ☐ ☐	☐ ☐ ☐ ☐ ☐
SUNDAY	☐ ☐ ☐ ☐ ☐	☐ ☐ ☐ ☐ ☐

WEEK:

This is our week to...

NAME:	NAME:

S
U
B
J
E
C
T
S

WEEK:

Weekly Planner

WEEK:

	NAME:	NAME:
MONDAY		
TUESDAY		
WEDNESDAY		
THURSDAY		
FRIDAY		
SATURDAY		
SUNDAY		

WEEK:

This is our week to... ______

NAME:	NAME:

SUBJECTS

WEEK:

Weekly Planner

WEEK:

	NAME:	NAME:
MONDAY	☐ ☐ ☐ ☐ ☐	☐ ☐ ☐ ☐ ☐
TUESDAY	☐ ☐ ☐ ☐ ☐	☐ ☐ ☐ ☐ ☐
WEDNESDAY	☐ ☐ ☐ ☐ ☐	☐ ☐ ☐ ☐ ☐
THURSDAY	☐ ☐ ☐ ☐ ☐	☐ ☐ ☐ ☐ ☐
FRIDAY	☐ ☐ ☐ ☐ ☐	☐ ☐ ☐ ☐ ☐
SATURDAY	☐ ☐ ☐ ☐ ☐	☐ ☐ ☐ ☐ ☐
SUNDAY	☐ ☐ ☐ ☐ ☐	☐ ☐ ☐ ☐ ☐

This is our week to... ____________________

NAME:	NAME:

SUBJECTS

WEEK:

Weekly Planner

WEEK:

	NAME:	NAME:
MONDAY		
TUESDAY		
WEDNESDAY		
THURSDAY		
FRIDAY		
SATURDAY		
SUNDAY		

WEEK:

This is our week to... ______________________

NAME:	NAME:

S U B J E C T S

WEEK:

Weekly Planner

WEEK: ____________________

	NAME:	NAME:
MONDAY	☐ ☐ ☐ ☐ ☐	☐ ☐ ☐ ☐ ☐
TUESDAY	☐ ☐ ☐ ☐ ☐	☐ ☐ ☐ ☐ ☐
WEDNESDAY	☐ ☐ ☐ ☐ ☐	☐ ☐ ☐ ☐ ☐
THURSDAY	☐ ☐ ☐ ☐ ☐	☐ ☐ ☐ ☐ ☐
FRIDAY	☐ ☐ ☐ ☐ ☐	☐ ☐ ☐ ☐ ☐
SATURDAY	☐ ☐ ☐ ☐ ☐	☐ ☐ ☐ ☐ ☐
SUNDAY	☐ ☐ ☐ ☐ ☐	☐ ☐ ☐ ☐ ☐

This is our week to...

NAME:	NAME:

SUBJECTS

WEEK:

Weekly Planner WEEK:

	NAME:	NAME:
MONDAY		
TUESDAY		
WEDNESDAY		
THURSDAY		
FRIDAY		
SATURDAY		
SUNDAY		

WEEK:

This is our week to... ______________________

NAME:	NAME:
☐	☐
☐	☐
☐	☐
☐	☐
☐	☐
☐	☐
☐	☐
☐	☐
☐	☐
☐	☐
☐	☐
☐	☐
☐	☐
☐	☐
☐	☐
☐	☐
☐	☐
☐	☐
☐	☐
☐	☐
☐	☐
☐	☐
☐	☐
☐	☐
☐	☐
☐	☐
☐	☐
☐	☐
☐	☐
☐	☐
☐	☐
☐	☐
☐	☐
☐	☐
☐	☐

S U B J E C T S

WEEK:

Weekly Planner

WEEK: ____________________

	NAME:	NAME:
MONDAY	☐ ☐ ☐ ☐ ☐	☐ ☐ ☐ ☐ ☐
TUESDAY	☐ ☐ ☐ ☐ ☐	☐ ☐ ☐ ☐ ☐
WEDNESDAY	☐ ☐ ☐ ☐ ☐	☐ ☐ ☐ ☐ ☐
THURSDAY	☐ ☐ ☐ ☐ ☐	☐ ☐ ☐ ☐ ☐
FRIDAY	☐ ☐ ☐ ☐ ☐	☐ ☐ ☐ ☐ ☐
SATURDAY	☐ ☐ ☐ ☐ ☐	☐ ☐ ☐ ☐ ☐
SUNDAY	☐ ☐ ☐ ☐ ☐	☐ ☐ ☐ ☐ ☐

This is our week to... ____________________

NAME:	NAME:

S
U
B
J
E
C
T
S

WEEK:

Weekly Planner

WEEK: ______________________

	NAME:	NAME:
MONDAY	☐ ☐ ☐ ☐ ☐	☐ ☐ ☐ ☐ ☐
TUESDAY	☐ ☐ ☐ ☐ ☐	☐ ☐ ☐ ☐ ☐
WEDNESDAY	☐ ☐ ☐ ☐ ☐	☐ ☐ ☐ ☐ ☐
THURSDAY	☐ ☐ ☐ ☐ ☐	☐ ☐ ☐ ☐ ☐
FRIDAY	☐ ☐ ☐ ☐ ☐	☐ ☐ ☐ ☐ ☐
SATURDAY	☐ ☐ ☐ ☐ ☐	☐ ☐ ☐ ☐ ☐
SUNDAY	☐ ☐ ☐ ☐ ☐	☐ ☐ ☐ ☐ ☐

WEEK:

This is our week to...

NAME:	NAME:

S U B J E C T S

WEEK:

Weekly Planner

WEEK: ______________________________

	NAME:	NAME:
MONDAY	☐ ☐ ☐ ☐ ☐	☐ ☐ ☐ ☐ ☐
TUESDAY	☐ ☐ ☐ ☐ ☐	☐ ☐ ☐ ☐ ☐
WEDNESDAY	☐ ☐ ☐ ☐ ☐	☐ ☐ ☐ ☐ ☐
THURSDAY	☐ ☐ ☐ ☐ ☐	☐ ☐ ☐ ☐ ☐
FRIDAY	☐ ☐ ☐ ☐ ☐	☐ ☐ ☐ ☐ ☐
SATURDAY	☐ ☐ ☐ ☐ ☐	☐ ☐ ☐ ☐ ☐
SUNDAY	☐ ☐ ☐ ☐ ☐	☐ ☐ ☐ ☐ ☐

WEEK:

This is our week to... ____________________

NAME:	NAME:
☐ ☐ ☐ ☐ ☐	☐ ☐ ☐ ☐ ☐
☐ ☐ ☐ ☐ ☐	☐ ☐ ☐ ☐ ☐
☐ ☐ ☐ ☐ ☐	☐ ☐ ☐ ☐ ☐
☐ ☐ ☐ ☐ ☐	☐ ☐ ☐ ☐ ☐
☐ ☐ ☐ ☐ ☐	☐ ☐ ☐ ☐ ☐
☐ ☐ ☐ ☐ ☐	☐ ☐ ☐ ☐ ☐
☐ ☐ ☐ ☐ ☐	☐ ☐ ☐ ☐ ☐

SUBJECTS

WEEK:

Weekly Planner

WEEK: ________

	NAME:	NAME:
MONDAY	☐ ☐ ☐ ☐ ☐	☐ ☐ ☐ ☐ ☐
TUESDAY	☐ ☐ ☐ ☐ ☐	☐ ☐ ☐ ☐ ☐
WEDNESDAY	☐ ☐ ☐ ☐ ☐	☐ ☐ ☐ ☐ ☐
THURSDAY	☐ ☐ ☐ ☐ ☐	☐ ☐ ☐ ☐ ☐
FRIDAY	☐ ☐ ☐ ☐ ☐	☐ ☐ ☐ ☐ ☐
SATURDAY	☐ ☐ ☐ ☐ ☐	☐ ☐ ☐ ☐ ☐
SUNDAY	☐ ☐ ☐ ☐ ☐	☐ ☐ ☐ ☐ ☐

WEEK:

This is our week to... ____________________

NAME:	NAME:
☐ ☐ ☐ ☐ ☐	☐ ☐ ☐ ☐ ☐
☐ ☐ ☐ ☐ ☐	☐ ☐ ☐ ☐ ☐
☐ ☐ ☐ ☐ ☐	☐ ☐ ☐ ☐ ☐
☐ ☐ ☐ ☐ ☐	☐ ☐ ☐ ☐ ☐
☐ ☐ ☐ ☐ ☐	☐ ☐ ☐ ☐ ☐
☐ ☐ ☐ ☐ ☐	☐ ☐ ☐ ☐ ☐
☐ ☐ ☐ ☐ ☐	☐ ☐ ☐ ☐ ☐

SUBJECTS

WEEK:

Weekly Planner

WEEK: ______

	NAME:	NAME:
MONDAY	☐ ☐ ☐ ☐ ☐	☐ ☐ ☐ ☐ ☐
TUESDAY	☐ ☐ ☐ ☐ ☐	☐ ☐ ☐ ☐ ☐
WEDNESDAY	☐ ☐ ☐ ☐ ☐	☐ ☐ ☐ ☐ ☐
THURSDAY	☐ ☐ ☐ ☐ ☐	☐ ☐ ☐ ☐ ☐
FRIDAY	☐ ☐ ☐ ☐ ☐	☐ ☐ ☐ ☐ ☐
SATURDAY	☐ ☐ ☐ ☐ ☐	☐ ☐ ☐ ☐ ☐
SUNDAY	☐ ☐ ☐ ☐ ☐	☐ ☐ ☐ ☐ ☐

WEEK:

This is our week to... ______________________

NAME:	NAME:

S U B J E C T S

WEEK:

Weekly Planner

WEEK: ____________________

	NAME:	NAME:
MONDAY	☐ ☐ ☐ ☐ ☐	☐ ☐ ☐ ☐ ☐
TUESDAY	☐ ☐ ☐ ☐ ☐	☐ ☐ ☐ ☐ ☐
WEDNESDAY	☐ ☐ ☐ ☐ ☐	☐ ☐ ☐ ☐ ☐
THURSDAY	☐ ☐ ☐ ☐ ☐	☐ ☐ ☐ ☐ ☐
FRIDAY	☐ ☐ ☐ ☐ ☐	☐ ☐ ☐ ☐ ☐
SATURDAY	☐ ☐ ☐ ☐ ☐	☐ ☐ ☐ ☐ ☐
SUNDAY	☐ ☐ ☐ ☐ ☐	☐ ☐ ☐ ☐ ☐

WEEK:

This is our week to...

NAME:	NAME:
☐ ☐ ☐ ☐ ☐	☐ ☐ ☐ ☐ ☐
☐ ☐ ☐ ☐ ☐	☐ ☐ ☐ ☐ ☐
☐ ☐ ☐ ☐ ☐	☐ ☐ ☐ ☐ ☐
☐ ☐ ☐ ☐ ☐	☐ ☐ ☐ ☐ ☐
☐ ☐ ☐ ☐ ☐	☐ ☐ ☐ ☐ ☐
☐ ☐ ☐ ☐ ☐	☐ ☐ ☐ ☐ ☐
☐ ☐ ☐ ☐ ☐	☐ ☐ ☐ ☐ ☐

SUBJECTS

WEEK:

Weekly Planner

WEEK:

	NAME:	NAME:
MONDAY		
TUESDAY		
WEDNESDAY		
THURSDAY		
FRIDAY		
SATURDAY		
SUNDAY		

WEEK:

This is our week to... ____________

NAME:	NAME:

S U B J E C T S

WEEK:

Weekly Planner

WEEK:

	NAME:	NAME:
MONDAY	☐ ☐ ☐ ☐ ☐	☐ ☐ ☐ ☐ ☐
TUESDAY	☐ ☐ ☐ ☐ ☐	☐ ☐ ☐ ☐ ☐
WEDNESDAY	☐ ☐ ☐ ☐ ☐	☐ ☐ ☐ ☐ ☐
THURSDAY	☐ ☐ ☐ ☐ ☐	☐ ☐ ☐ ☐ ☐
FRIDAY	☐ ☐ ☐ ☐ ☐	☐ ☐ ☐ ☐ ☐
SATURDAY	☐ ☐ ☐ ☐ ☐	☐ ☐ ☐ ☐ ☐
SUNDAY	☐ ☐ ☐ ☐ ☐	☐ ☐ ☐ ☐ ☐

WEEK:

This is our week to... ______________________

NAME:	NAME:
☐ ☐ ☐ ☐ ☐	☐ ☐ ☐ ☐ ☐
☐ ☐ ☐ ☐ ☐	☐ ☐ ☐ ☐ ☐
☐ ☐ ☐ ☐ ☐	☐ ☐ ☐ ☐ ☐
☐ ☐ ☐ ☐ ☐	☐ ☐ ☐ ☐ ☐
☐ ☐ ☐ ☐ ☐	☐ ☐ ☐ ☐ ☐
☐ ☐ ☐ ☐ ☐	☐ ☐ ☐ ☐ ☐
☐ ☐ ☐ ☐ ☐	☐ ☐ ☐ ☐ ☐

SUBJECTS

WEEK:

Weekly Planner

WEEK: ________

	NAME:	NAME:
MONDAY	☐ ☐ ☐ ☐ ☐	☐ ☐ ☐ ☐ ☐
TUESDAY	☐ ☐ ☐ ☐ ☐	☐ ☐ ☐ ☐ ☐
WEDNESDAY	☐ ☐ ☐ ☐ ☐	☐ ☐ ☐ ☐ ☐
THURSDAY	☐ ☐ ☐ ☐ ☐	☐ ☐ ☐ ☐ ☐
FRIDAY	☐ ☐ ☐ ☐ ☐	☐ ☐ ☐ ☐ ☐
SATURDAY	☐ ☐ ☐ ☐ ☐	☐ ☐ ☐ ☐ ☐
SUNDAY	☐ ☐ ☐ ☐ ☐	☐ ☐ ☐ ☐ ☐

WEEK:

This is our week to...

NAME:	NAME:

S U B J E C T S

WEEK:

Weekly Planner

WEEK: ______

	NAME:	NAME:
MONDAY	☐ ☐ ☐ ☐ ☐	☐ ☐ ☐ ☐ ☐
TUESDAY	☐ ☐ ☐ ☐ ☐	☐ ☐ ☐ ☐ ☐
WEDNESDAY	☐ ☐ ☐ ☐ ☐	☐ ☐ ☐ ☐ ☐
THURSDAY	☐ ☐ ☐ ☐ ☐	☐ ☐ ☐ ☐ ☐
FRIDAY	☐ ☐ ☐ ☐ ☐	☐ ☐ ☐ ☐ ☐
SATURDAY	☐ ☐ ☐ ☐ ☐	☐ ☐ ☐ ☐ ☐
SUNDAY	☐ ☐ ☐ ☐ ☐	☐ ☐ ☐ ☐ ☐

WEEK:

This is our week to... ______

NAME:	NAME:

SUBJECTS

WEEK:

Weekly Planner

WEEK: ____________________

	NAME:	NAME:
MONDAY	☐ ☐ ☐ ☐ ☐	☐ ☐ ☐ ☐ ☐
TUESDAY	☐ ☐ ☐ ☐ ☐	☐ ☐ ☐ ☐ ☐
WEDNESDAY	☐ ☐ ☐ ☐ ☐	☐ ☐ ☐ ☐ ☐
THURSDAY	☐ ☐ ☐ ☐ ☐	☐ ☐ ☐ ☐ ☐
FRIDAY	☐ ☐ ☐ ☐ ☐	☐ ☐ ☐ ☐ ☐
SATURDAY	☐ ☐ ☐ ☐ ☐	☐ ☐ ☐ ☐ ☐
SUNDAY	☐ ☐ ☐ ☐ ☐	☐ ☐ ☐ ☐ ☐

This is our week to... ______

NAME:	NAME:

S U B J E C T S

WEEK:

Weekly Planner

WEEK: ______

	NAME:	NAME:
MONDAY	☐ ☐ ☐ ☐ ☐	☐ ☐ ☐ ☐ ☐
TUESDAY	☐ ☐ ☐ ☐ ☐	☐ ☐ ☐ ☐ ☐
WEDNESDAY	☐ ☐ ☐ ☐ ☐	☐ ☐ ☐ ☐ ☐
THURSDAY	☐ ☐ ☐ ☐ ☐	☐ ☐ ☐ ☐ ☐
FRIDAY	☐ ☐ ☐ ☐ ☐	☐ ☐ ☐ ☐ ☐
SATURDAY	☐ ☐ ☐ ☐ ☐	☐ ☐ ☐ ☐ ☐
SUNDAY	☐ ☐ ☐ ☐ ☐	☐ ☐ ☐ ☐ ☐

WEEK:

This is our week to... ____________________

NAME:	NAME:

S U B J E C T S

WEEK:

Weekly Planner

WEEK: ______________________

	NAME:	NAME:
MONDAY	☐ ☐ ☐ ☐ ☐	☐ ☐ ☐ ☐ ☐
TUESDAY	☐ ☐ ☐ ☐ ☐	☐ ☐ ☐ ☐ ☐
WEDNESDAY	☐ ☐ ☐ ☐ ☐	☐ ☐ ☐ ☐ ☐
THURSDAY	☐ ☐ ☐ ☐ ☐	☐ ☐ ☐ ☐ ☐
FRIDAY	☐ ☐ ☐ ☐ ☐	☐ ☐ ☐ ☐ ☐
SATURDAY	☐ ☐ ☐ ☐ ☐	☐ ☐ ☐ ☐ ☐
SUNDAY	☐ ☐ ☐ ☐ ☐	☐ ☐ ☐ ☐ ☐

WEEK:

This is our week to... ___________

NAME:	NAME:

SUBJECTS

WEEK:

Weekly Planner

WEEK:

	NAME:	NAME:
MONDAY	☐ ☐ ☐ ☐ ☐	☐ ☐ ☐ ☐ ☐
TUESDAY	☐ ☐ ☐ ☐ ☐	☐ ☐ ☐ ☐ ☐
WEDNESDAY	☐ ☐ ☐ ☐ ☐	☐ ☐ ☐ ☐ ☐
THURSDAY	☐ ☐ ☐ ☐ ☐	☐ ☐ ☐ ☐ ☐
FRIDAY	☐ ☐ ☐ ☐ ☐	☐ ☐ ☐ ☐ ☐
SATURDAY	☐ ☐ ☐ ☐ ☐	☐ ☐ ☐ ☐ ☐
SUNDAY	☐ ☐ ☐ ☐ ☐	☐ ☐ ☐ ☐ ☐

WEEK:

This is our week to...

NAME:	NAME:

S U B J E C T S

WEEK:

Weekly Planner

WEEK: ______

	NAME:	NAME:
MONDAY	☐ ☐ ☐ ☐ ☐	☐ ☐ ☐ ☐ ☐
TUESDAY	☐ ☐ ☐ ☐ ☐	☐ ☐ ☐ ☐ ☐
WEDNESDAY	☐ ☐ ☐ ☐ ☐	☐ ☐ ☐ ☐ ☐
THURSDAY	☐ ☐ ☐ ☐ ☐	☐ ☐ ☐ ☐ ☐
FRIDAY	☐ ☐ ☐ ☐ ☐	☐ ☐ ☐ ☐ ☐
SATURDAY	☐ ☐ ☐ ☐ ☐	☐ ☐ ☐ ☐ ☐
SUNDAY	☐ ☐ ☐ ☐ ☐	☐ ☐ ☐ ☐ ☐

This is our week to...

NAME:	NAME:

SUBJECTS

WEEK:

Weekly Planner

WEEK: ____________________

	NAME:	NAME:
MONDAY		
TUESDAY		
WEDNESDAY		
THURSDAY		
FRIDAY		
SATURDAY		
SUNDAY		

WEEK:

This is our week to... ____________________

NAME:	NAME:
☐ ☐ ☐ ☐ ☐	☐ ☐ ☐ ☐ ☐
☐ ☐ ☐ ☐ ☐	☐ ☐ ☐ ☐ ☐
☐ ☐ ☐ ☐ ☐	☐ ☐ ☐ ☐ ☐
☐ ☐ ☐ ☐ ☐	☐ ☐ ☐ ☐ ☐
☐ ☐ ☐ ☐ ☐	☐ ☐ ☐ ☐ ☐
☐ ☐ ☐ ☐ ☐	☐ ☐ ☐ ☐ ☐
☐ ☐ ☐ ☐ ☐	☐ ☐ ☐ ☐ ☐

SUBJECTS

WEEK:

Weekly Planner

WEEK: ______________________

	NAME:	NAME:
MONDAY	☐ ☐ ☐ ☐ ☐	☐ ☐ ☐ ☐ ☐
TUESDAY	☐ ☐ ☐ ☐ ☐	☐ ☐ ☐ ☐ ☐
WEDNESDAY	☐ ☐ ☐ ☐ ☐	☐ ☐ ☐ ☐ ☐
THURSDAY	☐ ☐ ☐ ☐ ☐	☐ ☐ ☐ ☐ ☐
FRIDAY	☐ ☐ ☐ ☐ ☐	☐ ☐ ☐ ☐ ☐
SATURDAY	☐ ☐ ☐ ☐ ☐	☐ ☐ ☐ ☐ ☐
SUNDAY	☐ ☐ ☐ ☐ ☐	☐ ☐ ☐ ☐ ☐

This is our week to... ____________________

NAME:	NAME:
☐ ☐ ☐ ☐ ☐	☐ ☐ ☐ ☐ ☐
☐ ☐ ☐ ☐ ☐	☐ ☐ ☐ ☐ ☐
☐ ☐ ☐ ☐ ☐	☐ ☐ ☐ ☐ ☐
☐ ☐ ☐ ☐ ☐	☐ ☐ ☐ ☐ ☐
☐ ☐ ☐ ☐ ☐	☐ ☐ ☐ ☐ ☐
☐ ☐ ☐ ☐ ☐	☐ ☐ ☐ ☐ ☐
☐ ☐ ☐ ☐ ☐	☐ ☐ ☐ ☐ ☐

SUBJECTS

WEEK:

Weekly Planner

WEEK:

	NAME:	NAME:
MONDAY	☐ ☐ ☐ ☐ ☐	☐ ☐ ☐ ☐ ☐
TUESDAY	☐ ☐ ☐ ☐ ☐	☐ ☐ ☐ ☐ ☐
WEDNESDAY	☐ ☐ ☐ ☐ ☐	☐ ☐ ☐ ☐ ☐
THURSDAY	☐ ☐ ☐ ☐ ☐	☐ ☐ ☐ ☐ ☐
FRIDAY	☐ ☐ ☐ ☐ ☐	☐ ☐ ☐ ☐ ☐
SATURDAY	☐ ☐ ☐ ☐ ☐	☐ ☐ ☐ ☐ ☐
SUNDAY	☐ ☐ ☐ ☐ ☐	☐ ☐ ☐ ☐ ☐

This is our week to...

NAME:	NAME:

S U B J E C T S

WEEK:

Weekly Planner

WEEK: ______

	NAME:	NAME:
MONDAY	☐ ☐ ☐ ☐ ☐	☐ ☐ ☐ ☐ ☐
TUESDAY	☐ ☐ ☐ ☐ ☐	☐ ☐ ☐ ☐ ☐
WEDNESDAY	☐ ☐ ☐ ☐ ☐	☐ ☐ ☐ ☐ ☐
THURSDAY	☐ ☐ ☐ ☐ ☐	☐ ☐ ☐ ☐ ☐
FRIDAY	☐ ☐ ☐ ☐ ☐	☐ ☐ ☐ ☐ ☐
SATURDAY	☐ ☐ ☐ ☐ ☐	☐ ☐ ☐ ☐ ☐
SUNDAY	☐ ☐ ☐ ☐ ☐	☐ ☐ ☐ ☐ ☐

WEEK:

This is our week to... ______________________

NAME:	NAME:
☐ ☐ ☐ ☐ ☐	☐ ☐ ☐ ☐ ☐
☐ ☐ ☐ ☐ ☐	☐ ☐ ☐ ☐ ☐
☐ ☐ ☐ ☐ ☐	☐ ☐ ☐ ☐ ☐
☐ ☐ ☐ ☐ ☐	☐ ☐ ☐ ☐ ☐
☐ ☐ ☐ ☐ ☐	☐ ☐ ☐ ☐ ☐
☐ ☐ ☐ ☐ ☐	☐ ☐ ☐ ☐ ☐
☐ ☐ ☐ ☐ ☐	☐ ☐ ☐ ☐ ☐

SUBJECTS

WEEK:

Weekly Planner

WEEK: ____________________

	NAME:	NAME:
MONDAY	☐ ☐ ☐ ☐ ☐	☐ ☐ ☐ ☐ ☐
TUESDAY	☐ ☐ ☐ ☐ ☐	☐ ☐ ☐ ☐ ☐
WEDNESDAY	☐ ☐ ☐ ☐ ☐	☐ ☐ ☐ ☐ ☐
THURSDAY	☐ ☐ ☐ ☐ ☐	☐ ☐ ☐ ☐ ☐
FRIDAY	☐ ☐ ☐ ☐ ☐	☐ ☐ ☐ ☐ ☐
SATURDAY	☐ ☐ ☐ ☐ ☐	☐ ☐ ☐ ☐ ☐
SUNDAY	☐ ☐ ☐ ☐ ☐	☐ ☐ ☐ ☐ ☐

WEEK:

This is our week to... ____________________

NAME:	NAME:

S
U
B
J
E
C
T
S

WEEK:

Weekly Planner WEEK: ____________

	NAME:	NAME:
MONDAY	☐ ☐ ☐ ☐ ☐	☐ ☐ ☐ ☐ ☐
TUESDAY	☐ ☐ ☐ ☐ ☐	☐ ☐ ☐ ☐ ☐
WEDNESDAY	☐ ☐ ☐ ☐ ☐	☐ ☐ ☐ ☐ ☐
THURSDAY	☐ ☐ ☐ ☐ ☐	☐ ☐ ☐ ☐ ☐
FRIDAY	☐ ☐ ☐ ☐ ☐	☐ ☐ ☐ ☐ ☐
SATURDAY	☐ ☐ ☐ ☐ ☐	☐ ☐ ☐ ☐ ☐
SUNDAY	☐ ☐ ☐ ☐ ☐	☐ ☐ ☐ ☐ ☐

WEEK:

This is our week to...

NAME:	NAME:

S U B J E C T S

WEEK:

Weekly Planner

WEEK: ______

	NAME:	NAME:
MONDAY	☐ ☐ ☐ ☐ ☐	☐ ☐ ☐ ☐ ☐
TUESDAY	☐ ☐ ☐ ☐ ☐	☐ ☐ ☐ ☐ ☐
WEDNESDAY	☐ ☐ ☐ ☐ ☐	☐ ☐ ☐ ☐ ☐
THURSDAY	☐ ☐ ☐ ☐ ☐	☐ ☐ ☐ ☐ ☐
FRIDAY	☐ ☐ ☐ ☐ ☐	☐ ☐ ☐ ☐ ☐
SATURDAY	☐ ☐ ☐ ☐ ☐	☐ ☐ ☐ ☐ ☐
SUNDAY	☐ ☐ ☐ ☐ ☐	☐ ☐ ☐ ☐ ☐

WEEK:

This is our week to... ____________________

NAME:	NAME:

SUBJECTS

WEEK:

Weekly Planner

WEEK: ______

	NAME:	NAME:
MONDAY	☐ ☐ ☐ ☐ ☐	☐ ☐ ☐ ☐ ☐
TUESDAY	☐ ☐ ☐ ☐ ☐	☐ ☐ ☐ ☐ ☐
WEDNESDAY	☐ ☐ ☐ ☐ ☐	☐ ☐ ☐ ☐ ☐
THURSDAY	☐ ☐ ☐ ☐ ☐	☐ ☐ ☐ ☐ ☐
FRIDAY	☐ ☐ ☐ ☐ ☐	☐ ☐ ☐ ☐ ☐
SATURDAY	☐ ☐ ☐ ☐ ☐	☐ ☐ ☐ ☐ ☐
SUNDAY	☐ ☐ ☐ ☐ ☐	☐ ☐ ☐ ☐ ☐

WEEK:

This is our week to... ______________________

NAME:	NAME:

SUBJECTS

WEEK:

Weekly Planner

WEEK:

	NAME:	NAME:
MONDAY	☐ ☐ ☐ ☐ ☐	☐ ☐ ☐ ☐ ☐
TUESDAY	☐ ☐ ☐ ☐ ☐	☐ ☐ ☐ ☐ ☐
WEDNESDAY	☐ ☐ ☐ ☐ ☐	☐ ☐ ☐ ☐ ☐
THURSDAY	☐ ☐ ☐ ☐ ☐	☐ ☐ ☐ ☐ ☐
FRIDAY	☐ ☐ ☐ ☐ ☐	☐ ☐ ☐ ☐ ☐
SATURDAY	☐ ☐ ☐ ☐ ☐	☐ ☐ ☐ ☐ ☐
SUNDAY	☐ ☐ ☐ ☐ ☐	☐ ☐ ☐ ☐ ☐

This is our week to... ______________________

NAME:	NAME:
☐ ☐ ☐ ☐ ☐	☐ ☐ ☐ ☐ ☐
☐ ☐ ☐ ☐ ☐	☐ ☐ ☐ ☐ ☐
☐ ☐ ☐ ☐ ☐	☐ ☐ ☐ ☐ ☐
☐ ☐ ☐ ☐ ☐	☐ ☐ ☐ ☐ ☐
☐ ☐ ☐ ☐ ☐	☐ ☐ ☐ ☐ ☐
☐ ☐ ☐ ☐ ☐	☐ ☐ ☐ ☐ ☐
☐ ☐ ☐ ☐ ☐	☐ ☐ ☐ ☐ ☐

SUBJECTS

WEEK:

Weekly Planner

WEEK:

	NAME:	NAME:
MONDAY		
TUESDAY		
WEDNESDAY		
THURSDAY		
FRIDAY		
SATURDAY		
SUNDAY		

WEEK:

This is our week to... ______________________

NAME:	NAME:

S
U
B
J
E
C
T
S

WEEK:

Weekly Planner

WEEK: ____

	NAME:	NAME:
MONDAY	☐ ☐ ☐ ☐ ☐	☐ ☐ ☐ ☐ ☐
TUESDAY	☐ ☐ ☐ ☐ ☐	☐ ☐ ☐ ☐ ☐
WEDNESDAY	☐ ☐ ☐ ☐ ☐	☐ ☐ ☐ ☐ ☐
THURSDAY	☐ ☐ ☐ ☐ ☐	☐ ☐ ☐ ☐ ☐
FRIDAY	☐ ☐ ☐ ☐ ☐	☐ ☐ ☐ ☐ ☐
SATURDAY	☐ ☐ ☐ ☐ ☐	☐ ☐ ☐ ☐ ☐
SUNDAY	☐ ☐ ☐ ☐ ☐	☐ ☐ ☐ ☐ ☐

WEEK:

This is our week to... ______________________

NAME:	NAME:

SUBJECTS

WEEK:

Weekly Planner

WEEK: ____________________

	NAME:	NAME:
MONDAY	☐ ☐ ☐ ☐ ☐	☐ ☐ ☐ ☐ ☐
TUESDAY	☐ ☐ ☐ ☐ ☐	☐ ☐ ☐ ☐ ☐
WEDNESDAY	☐ ☐ ☐ ☐ ☐	☐ ☐ ☐ ☐ ☐
THURSDAY	☐ ☐ ☐ ☐ ☐	☐ ☐ ☐ ☐ ☐
FRIDAY	☐ ☐ ☐ ☐ ☐	☐ ☐ ☐ ☐ ☐
SATURDAY	☐ ☐ ☐ ☐ ☐	☐ ☐ ☐ ☐ ☐
SUNDAY	☐ ☐ ☐ ☐ ☐	☐ ☐ ☐ ☐ ☐

WEEK:

This is our week to...

NAME:	NAME:

SUBJECTS

WEEK:

Weekly Planner

WEEK:

	NAME:	NAME:
MONDAY		
TUESDAY		
WEDNESDAY		
THURSDAY		
FRIDAY		
SATURDAY		
SUNDAY		

WEEK:

This is our week to... ____________________

NAME:	NAME:
☐ ☐ ☐ ☐ ☐	☐ ☐ ☐ ☐ ☐
☐ ☐ ☐ ☐ ☐	☐ ☐ ☐ ☐ ☐
☐ ☐ ☐ ☐ ☐	☐ ☐ ☐ ☐ ☐
☐ ☐ ☐ ☐ ☐	☐ ☐ ☐ ☐ ☐
☐ ☐ ☐ ☐ ☐	☐ ☐ ☐ ☐ ☐
☐ ☐ ☐ ☐ ☐	☐ ☐ ☐ ☐ ☐
☐ ☐ ☐ ☐ ☐	☐ ☐ ☐ ☐ ☐

SUBJECTS

WEEK:

Weekly Planner

WEEK: ____________________

	NAME:	NAME:
MONDAY	☐ ☐ ☐ ☐ ☐	☐ ☐ ☐ ☐ ☐
TUESDAY	☐ ☐ ☐ ☐ ☐	☐ ☐ ☐ ☐ ☐
WEDNESDAY	☐ ☐ ☐ ☐ ☐	☐ ☐ ☐ ☐ ☐
THURSDAY	☐ ☐ ☐ ☐ ☐	☐ ☐ ☐ ☐ ☐
FRIDAY	☐ ☐ ☐ ☐ ☐	☐ ☐ ☐ ☐ ☐
SATURDAY	☐ ☐ ☐ ☐ ☐	☐ ☐ ☐ ☐ ☐
SUNDAY	☐ ☐ ☐ ☐ ☐	☐ ☐ ☐ ☐ ☐

WEEK:

This is our week to... ____________________

NAME:	NAME:
☐ ☐ ☐ ☐ ☐	☐ ☐ ☐ ☐ ☐
☐ ☐ ☐ ☐ ☐	☐ ☐ ☐ ☐ ☐
☐ ☐ ☐ ☐ ☐	☐ ☐ ☐ ☐ ☐
☐ ☐ ☐ ☐ ☐	☐ ☐ ☐ ☐ ☐
☐ ☐ ☐ ☐ ☐	☐ ☐ ☐ ☐ ☐
☐ ☐ ☐ ☐ ☐	☐ ☐ ☐ ☐ ☐
☐ ☐ ☐ ☐ ☐	☐ ☐ ☐ ☐ ☐

SUBJECTS

WEEK:

Weekly Planner

WEEK: ______

	NAME:	NAME:
MONDAY	☐ ☐ ☐ ☐ ☐	☐ ☐ ☐ ☐ ☐
TUESDAY	☐ ☐ ☐ ☐ ☐	☐ ☐ ☐ ☐ ☐
WEDNESDAY	☐ ☐ ☐ ☐ ☐	☐ ☐ ☐ ☐ ☐
THURSDAY	☐ ☐ ☐ ☐ ☐	☐ ☐ ☐ ☐ ☐
FRIDAY	☐ ☐ ☐ ☐ ☐	☐ ☐ ☐ ☐ ☐
SATURDAY	☐ ☐ ☐ ☐ ☐	☐ ☐ ☐ ☐ ☐
SUNDAY	☐ ☐ ☐ ☐ ☐	☐ ☐ ☐ ☐ ☐

WEEK:

This is our week to...

NAME:	NAME:

SUBJECTS

WEEK:

Weekly Planner

WEEK: ______

	NAME:	NAME:
MONDAY		
TUESDAY		
WEDNESDAY		
THURSDAY		
FRIDAY		
SATURDAY		
SUNDAY		

WEEK:

This is our week to... ______________________

NAME:	NAME:
☐ ☐ ☐ ☐ ☐	☐ ☐ ☐ ☐ ☐
☐ ☐ ☐ ☐ ☐	☐ ☐ ☐ ☐ ☐
☐ ☐ ☐ ☐ ☐	☐ ☐ ☐ ☐ ☐
☐ ☐ ☐ ☐ ☐	☐ ☐ ☐ ☐ ☐
☐ ☐ ☐ ☐ ☐	☐ ☐ ☐ ☐ ☐
☐ ☐ ☐ ☐ ☐	☐ ☐ ☐ ☐ ☐
☐ ☐ ☐ ☐ ☐	☐ ☐ ☐ ☐ ☐

SUBJECTS

WEEK:

Weekly Planner

WEEK:

	NAME:	NAME:
MONDAY		
TUESDAY		
WEDNESDAY		
THURSDAY		
FRIDAY		
SATURDAY		
SUNDAY		

WEEK:

This is our week to... ______________________

NAME:	NAME:
☐ ☐ ☐ ☐ ☐	☐ ☐ ☐ ☐ ☐
☐ ☐ ☐ ☐ ☐	☐ ☐ ☐ ☐ ☐
☐ ☐ ☐ ☐ ☐	☐ ☐ ☐ ☐ ☐
☐ ☐ ☐ ☐ ☐	☐ ☐ ☐ ☐ ☐
☐ ☐ ☐ ☐ ☐	☐ ☐ ☐ ☐ ☐
☐ ☐ ☐ ☐ ☐	☐ ☐ ☐ ☐ ☐
☐ ☐ ☐ ☐ ☐	☐ ☐ ☐ ☐ ☐

SUBJECTS

WEEK:

Weekly Planner

WEEK: ____

	NAME:	NAME:
MONDAY	☐ ☐ ☐ ☐ ☐	☐ ☐ ☐ ☐ ☐
TUESDAY	☐ ☐ ☐ ☐ ☐	☐ ☐ ☐ ☐ ☐
WEDNESDAY	☐ ☐ ☐ ☐ ☐	☐ ☐ ☐ ☐ ☐
THURSDAY	☐ ☐ ☐ ☐ ☐	☐ ☐ ☐ ☐ ☐
FRIDAY	☐ ☐ ☐ ☐ ☐	☐ ☐ ☐ ☐ ☐
SATURDAY	☐ ☐ ☐ ☐ ☐	☐ ☐ ☐ ☐ ☐
SUNDAY	☐ ☐ ☐ ☐ ☐	☐ ☐ ☐ ☐ ☐

WEEK:

This is our week to...

NAME:	NAME:

SUBJECTS

WEEK:

Weekly Planner

WEEK: ____

	NAME:	NAME:
MONDAY	☐ ☐ ☐ ☐ ☐	☐ ☐ ☐ ☐ ☐
TUESDAY	☐ ☐ ☐ ☐ ☐	☐ ☐ ☐ ☐ ☐
WEDNESDAY	☐ ☐ ☐ ☐ ☐	☐ ☐ ☐ ☐ ☐
THURSDAY	☐ ☐ ☐ ☐ ☐	☐ ☐ ☐ ☐ ☐
FRIDAY	☐ ☐ ☐ ☐ ☐	☐ ☐ ☐ ☐ ☐
SATURDAY	☐ ☐ ☐ ☐ ☐	☐ ☐ ☐ ☐ ☐
SUNDAY	☐ ☐ ☐ ☐ ☐	☐ ☐ ☐ ☐ ☐

This is our week to... ______________________

NAME:	NAME:

SUBJECTS

WEEK:

Weekly Planner

WEEK: ____________________

	NAME:	NAME:
MONDAY	☐ ☐ ☐ ☐ ☐	☐ ☐ ☐ ☐ ☐
TUESDAY	☐ ☐ ☐ ☐ ☐	☐ ☐ ☐ ☐ ☐
WEDNESDAY	☐ ☐ ☐ ☐ ☐	☐ ☐ ☐ ☐ ☐
THURSDAY	☐ ☐ ☐ ☐ ☐	☐ ☐ ☐ ☐ ☐
FRIDAY	☐ ☐ ☐ ☐ ☐	☐ ☐ ☐ ☐ ☐
SATURDAY	☐ ☐ ☐ ☐ ☐	☐ ☐ ☐ ☐ ☐
SUNDAY	☐ ☐ ☐ ☐ ☐	☐ ☐ ☐ ☐ ☐

WEEK:

This is our week to... ______________________

NAME:	NAME:
☐ ☐ ☐ ☐ ☐	☐ ☐ ☐ ☐ ☐
☐ ☐ ☐ ☐ ☐	☐ ☐ ☐ ☐ ☐
☐ ☐ ☐ ☐ ☐	☐ ☐ ☐ ☐ ☐
☐ ☐ ☐ ☐ ☐	☐ ☐ ☐ ☐ ☐
☐ ☐ ☐ ☐ ☐	☐ ☐ ☐ ☐ ☐
☐ ☐ ☐ ☐ ☐	☐ ☐ ☐ ☐ ☐
☐ ☐ ☐ ☐ ☐	☐ ☐ ☐ ☐ ☐

SUBJECTS

WEEK:

Weekly Planner WEEK: ______

	NAME:	NAME:
MONDAY	☐ ☐ ☐ ☐ ☐	☐ ☐ ☐ ☐ ☐
TUESDAY	☐ ☐ ☐ ☐ ☐	☐ ☐ ☐ ☐ ☐
WEDNESDAY	☐ ☐ ☐ ☐ ☐	☐ ☐ ☐ ☐ ☐
THURSDAY	☐ ☐ ☐ ☐ ☐	☐ ☐ ☐ ☐ ☐
FRIDAY	☐ ☐ ☐ ☐ ☐	☐ ☐ ☐ ☐ ☐
SATURDAY	☐ ☐ ☐ ☐ ☐	☐ ☐ ☐ ☐ ☐
SUNDAY	☐ ☐ ☐ ☐ ☐	☐ ☐ ☐ ☐ ☐

WEEK:

This is our week to... ______________________________

NAME:	NAME:
☐ ☐ ☐ ☐ ☐	☐ ☐ ☐ ☐ ☐
☐ ☐ ☐ ☐ ☐	☐ ☐ ☐ ☐ ☐
☐ ☐ ☐ ☐ ☐	☐ ☐ ☐ ☐ ☐
☐ ☐ ☐ ☐ ☐	☐ ☐ ☐ ☐ ☐
☐ ☐ ☐ ☐ ☐	☐ ☐ ☐ ☐ ☐
☐ ☐ ☐ ☐ ☐	☐ ☐ ☐ ☐ ☐
☐ ☐ ☐ ☐ ☐	☐ ☐ ☐ ☐ ☐

SUBJECTS

WEEK:

Weekly Planner

WEEK: ________________

	NAME:	NAME:
MONDAY	☐ ☐ ☐ ☐ ☐	☐ ☐ ☐ ☐ ☐
TUESDAY	☐ ☐ ☐ ☐ ☐	☐ ☐ ☐ ☐ ☐
WEDNESDAY	☐ ☐ ☐ ☐ ☐	☐ ☐ ☐ ☐ ☐
THURSDAY	☐ ☐ ☐ ☐ ☐	☐ ☐ ☐ ☐ ☐
FRIDAY	☐ ☐ ☐ ☐ ☐	☐ ☐ ☐ ☐ ☐
SATURDAY	☐ ☐ ☐ ☐ ☐	☐ ☐ ☐ ☐ ☐
SUNDAY	☐ ☐ ☐ ☐ ☐	☐ ☐ ☐ ☐ ☐

WEEK:

This is our week to...

NAME:	NAME:
☐ ☐ ☐ ☐ ☐	☐ ☐ ☐ ☐ ☐
☐ ☐ ☐ ☐ ☐	☐ ☐ ☐ ☐ ☐
☐ ☐ ☐ ☐ ☐	☐ ☐ ☐ ☐ ☐
☐ ☐ ☐ ☐ ☐	☐ ☐ ☐ ☐ ☐
☐ ☐ ☐ ☐ ☐	☐ ☐ ☐ ☐ ☐
☐ ☐ ☐ ☐ ☐	☐ ☐ ☐ ☐ ☐
☐ ☐ ☐ ☐ ☐	☐ ☐ ☐ ☐ ☐

SUBJECTS

WEEK:

Weekly Planner

WEEK: ____________________

	NAME:	NAME:
MONDAY	☐ ☐ ☐ ☐ ☐	☐ ☐ ☐ ☐ ☐
TUESDAY	☐ ☐ ☐ ☐ ☐	☐ ☐ ☐ ☐ ☐
WEDNESDAY	☐ ☐ ☐ ☐ ☐	☐ ☐ ☐ ☐ ☐
THURSDAY	☐ ☐ ☐ ☐ ☐	☐ ☐ ☐ ☐ ☐
FRIDAY	☐ ☐ ☐ ☐ ☐	☐ ☐ ☐ ☐ ☐
SATURDAY	☐ ☐ ☐ ☐ ☐	☐ ☐ ☐ ☐ ☐
SUNDAY	☐ ☐ ☐ ☐ ☐	☐ ☐ ☐ ☐ ☐

This is our week to...

NAME:	NAME:

S
U
B
J
E
C
T
S

WEEK:

Weekly Planner WEEK:

	NAME:	NAME:
MONDAY		
TUESDAY		
WEDNESDAY		
THURSDAY		
FRIDAY		
SATURDAY		
SUNDAY		

WEEK:

This is our week to... ______________________

NAME:	NAME:

SUBJECTS

WEEK:

Weekly Planner

WEEK: ______________________

	NAME:	NAME:
MONDAY	☐ ☐ ☐ ☐ ☐	☐ ☐ ☐ ☐ ☐
TUESDAY	☐ ☐ ☐ ☐ ☐	☐ ☐ ☐ ☐ ☐
WEDNESDAY	☐ ☐ ☐ ☐ ☐	☐ ☐ ☐ ☐ ☐
THURSDAY	☐ ☐ ☐ ☐ ☐	☐ ☐ ☐ ☐ ☐
FRIDAY	☐ ☐ ☐ ☐ ☐	☐ ☐ ☐ ☐ ☐
SATURDAY	☐ ☐ ☐ ☐ ☐	☐ ☐ ☐ ☐ ☐
SUNDAY	☐ ☐ ☐ ☐ ☐	☐ ☐ ☐ ☐ ☐

WEEK:

This is our week to... ______________________

NAME:	NAME:
☐ ☐ ☐ ☐ ☐	☐ ☐ ☐ ☐ ☐
☐ ☐ ☐ ☐ ☐	☐ ☐ ☐ ☐ ☐
☐ ☐ ☐ ☐ ☐	☐ ☐ ☐ ☐ ☐
☐ ☐ ☐ ☐ ☐	☐ ☐ ☐ ☐ ☐
☐ ☐ ☐ ☐ ☐	☐ ☐ ☐ ☐ ☐
☐ ☐ ☐ ☐ ☐	☐ ☐ ☐ ☐ ☐
☐ ☐ ☐ ☐ ☐	☐ ☐ ☐ ☐ ☐

SUBJECTS

WEEK:

Weekly Planner

WEEK:

	NAME:	NAME:
MONDAY		
TUESDAY		
WEDNESDAY		
THURSDAY		
FRIDAY		
SATURDAY		
SUNDAY		

WEEK:

This is our week to...

NAME:	NAME:
☐ ☐ ☐ ☐ ☐	☐ ☐ ☐ ☐ ☐
☐ ☐ ☐ ☐ ☐	☐ ☐ ☐ ☐ ☐
☐ ☐ ☐ ☐ ☐	☐ ☐ ☐ ☐ ☐
☐ ☐ ☐ ☐ ☐	☐ ☐ ☐ ☐ ☐
☐ ☐ ☐ ☐ ☐	☐ ☐ ☐ ☐ ☐
☐ ☐ ☐ ☐ ☐	☐ ☐ ☐ ☐ ☐
☐ ☐ ☐ ☐ ☐	☐ ☐ ☐ ☐ ☐

SUBJECTS

WEEK:

Weekly Planner

WEEK:

	NAME:	NAME:
MONDAY	☐ ☐ ☐ ☐ ☐	☐ ☐ ☐ ☐ ☐
TUESDAY	☐ ☐ ☐ ☐ ☐	☐ ☐ ☐ ☐ ☐
WEDNESDAY	☐ ☐ ☐ ☐ ☐	☐ ☐ ☐ ☐ ☐
THURSDAY	☐ ☐ ☐ ☐ ☐	☐ ☐ ☐ ☐ ☐
FRIDAY	☐ ☐ ☐ ☐ ☐	☐ ☐ ☐ ☐ ☐
SATURDAY	☐ ☐ ☐ ☐ ☐	☐ ☐ ☐ ☐ ☐
SUNDAY	☐ ☐ ☐ ☐ ☐	☐ ☐ ☐ ☐ ☐

WEEK:

This is our week to... ____________________

NAME:	NAME:
☐ ☐ ☐ ☐ ☐	☐ ☐ ☐ ☐ ☐
☐ ☐ ☐ ☐ ☐	☐ ☐ ☐ ☐ ☐
☐ ☐ ☐ ☐ ☐	☐ ☐ ☐ ☐ ☐
☐ ☐ ☐ ☐ ☐	☐ ☐ ☐ ☐ ☐
☐ ☐ ☐ ☐ ☐	☐ ☐ ☐ ☐ ☐
☐ ☐ ☐ ☐ ☐	☐ ☐ ☐ ☐ ☐
☐ ☐ ☐ ☐ ☐	☐ ☐ ☐ ☐ ☐

SUBJECTS

WEEK:

Weekly Planner

WEEK: ____

	NAME:	NAME:
MONDAY	☐ ☐ ☐ ☐ ☐	☐ ☐ ☐ ☐ ☐
TUESDAY	☐ ☐ ☐ ☐ ☐	☐ ☐ ☐ ☐ ☐
WEDNESDAY	☐ ☐ ☐ ☐ ☐	☐ ☐ ☐ ☐ ☐
THURSDAY	☐ ☐ ☐ ☐ ☐	☐ ☐ ☐ ☐ ☐
FRIDAY	☐ ☐ ☐ ☐ ☐	☐ ☐ ☐ ☐ ☐
SATURDAY	☐ ☐ ☐ ☐ ☐	☐ ☐ ☐ ☐ ☐
SUNDAY	☐ ☐ ☐ ☐ ☐	☐ ☐ ☐ ☐ ☐

This is our week to... ______________________

NAME:	NAME:
☐ ☐ ☐ ☐ ☐	☐ ☐ ☐ ☐ ☐
☐ ☐ ☐ ☐ ☐	☐ ☐ ☐ ☐ ☐
☐ ☐ ☐ ☐ ☐	☐ ☐ ☐ ☐ ☐
☐ ☐ ☐ ☐ ☐	☐ ☐ ☐ ☐ ☐
☐ ☐ ☐ ☐ ☐	☐ ☐ ☐ ☐ ☐
☐ ☐ ☐ ☐ ☐	☐ ☐ ☐ ☐ ☐
☐ ☐ ☐ ☐ ☐	☐ ☐ ☐ ☐ ☐

S U B J E C T S

WEEK:

Weekly Planner

WEEK:

	NAME:	NAME:
MONDAY	☐ ☐ ☐ ☐ ☐	☐ ☐ ☐ ☐ ☐
TUESDAY	☐ ☐ ☐ ☐ ☐	☐ ☐ ☐ ☐ ☐
WEDNESDAY	☐ ☐ ☐ ☐ ☐	☐ ☐ ☐ ☐ ☐
THURSDAY	☐ ☐ ☐ ☐ ☐	☐ ☐ ☐ ☐ ☐
FRIDAY	☐ ☐ ☐ ☐ ☐	☐ ☐ ☐ ☐ ☐
SATURDAY	☐ ☐ ☐ ☐ ☐	☐ ☐ ☐ ☐ ☐
SUNDAY	☐ ☐ ☐ ☐ ☐	☐ ☐ ☐ ☐ ☐

WEEK:

This is our week to... ______________________

NAME:	NAME:
☐	☐
☐	☐
☐	☐
☐	☐
☐	☐

SUBJECTS

WEEK:

	SUBJECT	ASSIGNMENT	MILESTONE

GRADES & MILESTONES

Strive for progress not perfection

GRADE	DATE ACHIEVED	COMMENTS

GRADES & MILESTONES

	SUBJECT	ASSIGNMENT	MILESTONE

GRADES & MILESTONES

Strive for progress not perfection

GRADE	DATE ACHIEVED	COMMENTS

GRADES & MILESTONES

	SUBJECT	ASSIGNMENT	MILESTONE

Strive for progress not perfection

GRADE	DATE ACHIEVED	COMMENTS

GRADES & MILESTONES

	SUBJECT	ASSIGNMENT	MILESTONE

GRADES & MILESTONES

Strive for progress not perfection

GRADE	DATE ACHIEVED	COMMENTS

GRADES & MILESTONES

Year in Review

YEAR: ____________________

MY YEAR IN REVIEW

YEAR IN REVIEW

Notes

Notes

Made in the USA
San Bernardino, CA
11 August 2020